The Suffering Paradox

Keithen Hamilton

En Route Books and Media, LLC
Saint Louis, MO

⊕ *ENROUTE*
Make the time

En Route Books and Media, LLC
5705 Rhodes Avenue
St. Louis, MO 63109

Contact us at
contactus@enroutebooksandmedia.com

Cover art by Keithen Hamilton using DALL-E
Copyright 2025 Keithen Hamilton

ISBN: 979-8-88870-412-7
Library of Congress Control Number:
Available online at https://catalog.loc.gov

All rights reserved. No part of this book may be reproduced, stored in a retrieval system, or transmitted in any form, or by any means, electronic, mechanical, photocopying, or otherwise, without the prior written permission of the author.

Table of Contents

Chapter 1: Our Thoughts 1
    A Modern Understanding 3
    A Western Understanding 5
    An Ancient Understanding 8
    Don't Forget the East 13

Chapter 2: Our Stories 17
    A Diving Adventure 18
    A Good Old Fashioned Poor-Off 22
    First Responders 25

Chapter 3: The Effects 37
    The Psychological Impact of Suffering 39
    The Neurological Correlates of Endurance 42
    The Sociocultural Benefits of Collective
        Struggle 46
    The Paradox of Comfort 49
    Suffering as a Prerequisite for Fulfillment 52
    Out of Studies into Stories 54

Chapter 4: Transcendentals 57
Goodness 58
Truth 67
Beauty 70
Suffering 72

Chapter 5: The Paradox and its Elimination 75
Death of Definitions 77

Chapter 6: The Problem of Evil 89
The Arguments: 95
The Logical Problem of Evil 96
The Evidential Problem of Evil 97
The Problem of Natural Evil 100
The Suffering of the Innocent 101

About the Author 105

Chapter 1

Our Thoughts

"If you are distressed by anything external, the pain is not due to the thing itself, but to your estimate of it; and this you have the power to revoke at any moment."

-Marcus Aurelius

How do you define suffering? I want you to take a few minutes to really contemplate this question and write your answer at the top of this page. You'll be able to revisit it throughout your time in this book.

It is one of those words that we all think we know…until our kids (or some random author) ask us to define it. Suffering is a universally recognized experience, yet its definition can be elusive and difficult to articulate. One basic principle of suffering we all can agree on is that suffering is negative…right?

The problem of evil is exemplified in suffering. It is a state we wish to avoid, encompassing a wide range of negative experiences, both physical and emotional. Pain, distress, anguish, loss, longing for love, frustration, torture, illness, and disease are all manifestations of suffering. It signals that something is amiss and needs to be rectified. A benevolent God would never christen a world if it contained such a monstrosity. We can all agree the modern goal is to eliminate unnecessary or unwanted suffering the best we can.

Paradoxically, we see time and time again that the embodiment of living is accomplished by those who embrace and immerse themselves in suffering. The stories that we read, the infatuation and fixation on the words of those who speak, and the accomplishments we celebrate are of the men who do not shy away from their suffering. This is an indication that suffering is as an ordering of good, a tool of the benevolent being.

This is the paradox, as much as we have come to know suffering as bad, can we also come to know suffering as good? Is it possible that we do not understand this overly used and abused word as much as we think?

A Modern Understanding

It exists in as pervasive a manner today as it did millennia ago. In one way or another, it is easily the number one subject on everyone's mind. The desire to alleviate suffering is a deep-rooted theme in contemporary society. It dominates public discourse, social media, and political agendas. Regardless of one's stance on any issue, the ultimate goal is often to reduce suffering for a particular group. However, this inevitably involves choosing which group will bear the burden of suffering and to what extent. That, in itself, puts you in a state of suffering. How do we balance the suffering?

Do we focus on the environment? Increase minor suffering now to reduce major suffering in the future? Do we choose an economic system that increases suffering for the majority but balances it equally across the range of human abilities and circumstances? Do we prefer the economic system that reduces the average but permits both extremes? Is the cure worse than the disease? Should a certain drug be banned? Does that drug relieve suffering in society or increase suffering? Does it reduce the suffering for an individual while increasing the suffering of the community?

What about the availability of the opposite? Comfort, assuming comfort is the opposite, is our number one purchase. The pursuit of comfort is a defining characteristic of our modern life—whether that purchase is a bed and recliner or pain pills and hallucinogens.

Television and video games allow us to escape our world and enter the make believe. What is this if not an escape from our own suffering? We put ourselves through the suffering of exercise to reduce suffering later in life. Maybe we exercise to gain attraction to escape the suffering of loneliness.

Modern medicine has made the pursuit of comfort a central focus. It has developed an impressive arsenal to address various states of discomfort. This includes a wide array of pain relievers, an entire medical specialty dedicated to pain management, and advanced techniques to treat and cure a vast range of ailments. Additionally, the field of psychology has made significant strides in addressing the symptoms of suffering, such as anxiety, depression, and addiction. The overarching goal of these medical and psychological interventions is to alleviate suffering and restore a state of comfort and well-being.

Regardless of the topic, the reductionist view of our modern goal is to reduce suffering to the lowest possible level. Why? Our modern understanding of suffering is that it stems from evil. Perhaps personifies evil. While it serves a purpose, it is inherently negative; its primary characteristic is its detrimental impact on individuals and society. Is this the historical or classical view of suffering?

A Western Understanding

To fully comprehend the nature of suffering, it is essential to consider diverse perspectives and historical contexts. Was there a major shift in thought towards suffering during the Enlightenment period or the Renaissance?

The great thinkers of the Enlightenment period championed the revival of individualism and the shift of our thought towards what they defined as rationality. This change in philosophy, though not entirely novel, led to our focus on reducing negative human experiences as a collective through and driven by the individual. This subtle but important difference sought to minimize human suffering through collective action driven by individual initiative. Your burden is lifted so you can lift the burden of those around you. They then could do the same, and, thus, a virtuous cycle would be born. These concepts fueled the French and American Revolution. As John Stuart Mill wrote, 'The worth of a state, in the long run, is the worth of the individuals composing it.'

As odd as it may sound, both Communism and Capitalism, despite their contrasting ideologies, stemmed from this line of reasoning. As Karl Marx wrote, 'The free development of each is the condition for the free development of all.' Both sought to minimize suffering, Capitalism by empowering the individual to generate prosperity, and Communism by attempting to ensure collective equity and security. This is the root of our modern understanding; thus, it agrees wholeheartedly with our modern interpretation. Suffering is an evil, and it should be negated as much as possible.

While this was the goal of the Enlightenment era, it was less the target and more the by-product during the Middle Ages. The Middle Ages, heavily influenced by Christianity, saw suffering as inherently evil but with a divine purpose: atonement, penance, and a consequence of humanity's fallen nature. This persists as the argument used by Christianity to this day. It was a necessary evil, utilized by God to achieve greater good than that which could be achieved without it. Jesus's redemptive act served as an example for all to embrace suffering. Jesus's redemptive act was suffering. Through embracing our suffering, we could bring greater good than what could have otherwise been achieved. Thus, we should not avoid this suffering at all; instead, we should embrace and subjugate it to our benefit, increasing our knowledge and piety. While the results do decrease suffering, it wasn't the main goal. This may seem very positive, but the word was still negative. How we treated it may have been very different, but our thoughts were still ones of evil.

As we move back into the latter half of the first millennium, we find it, too, was heavily rooted in Christian belief. St Augustine believed much of what we already covered, and St. Thomas Aquinas built upon his works and influenced Medieval thought. Within Christian thought, however, we see a subtly distinct difference. The Apostle Paul described suffering as an inevitable opportunity to share in Christ's suffering. This stands alone as the first true divergence from suffering being inherently evil. While in a more intricate and subtle manner he didn't appear to see suffering as evil, he did appear to have seen suffering as a good and natural opportunity and invitation to live as Jesus did.

An Ancient Understanding

Judaism, being the roots of Christianity, holds a similar but more complex perspective on suffering. While ancient Jewish writings on the topic appeared to be scarce in my research, their beliefs have significantly influenced Christian thought. Both religions generally perceive suffering as an evil consequence of humanity's separation from God due to sin. However, a key distinction lies in the concept of "test of faith," which is more prominent in Judaism but does exist within Christianity.

Jewish tradition, as exemplified in the Book of Job, maintains that even the righteous will suffer, and this suffering serves as a trial of their faith. While suffering is fundamentally evil, it can also be a divine instrument for testing and refining one's devotion to God.

A notable exception to the view of suffering as purely evil is found in Jewish mystical and wisdom traditions that describe suffering as disciplinary (cf. Prov 3:11-12; Heb 12:5-11) and purposeful, showing that God can bring good out of it. This mystical tradition within Judaism proposes that suffering can have redemptive qualities, acting as a catalyst for the restoration and ultimate redemption of the world. This concept suggests that suffering is less inherently negative and is transformed into a force for positive change and spiritual growth.

The millennium preceding the spread of Christianity and the subsequent convergence of philosophical and theological thought gave rise to a richer and more nuanced comprehension of suffering. Greek and Roman perspectives on suffering were diverse and complex, ranging from the notion of suffering as pure evil inflicted by capricious gods upon humanity for their amusement to the concept of suffering as an inevitable consequence of human actions. This spectrum of beliefs is evident in the great epics and tragic hero narratives, where divine entities torment the protagonist or where the hero's suffering stems from their hubris, often referred to as fate.

In one perspective, suffering was perceived as the ultimate evil, a manifestation of the strong exploiting the weak. Conversely, another viewpoint posited that suffering was inherently neither good nor bad, but rather a natural consequence to be overcome through adherence to principles. These divergent perspectives gave rise to a multitude of philosophical schools of thought on suffering, with Stoicism and Epicureanism representing two contrasting extremes.

Please keep in mind that this is only a quick and superficial look at a very complicated topic. The complexities of Stoic and Epicurean philosophies, as well as the countless other schools of thought from this period, cannot be adequately explored here, especially by me.

Stoicism, a school of philosophy that originated in ancient Greece, placed a strong emphasis on the individual's state of mind rather than on external circumstances, including suffering. The Stoics believed that one's internal state determined whether they were truly suffering, regardless of their external situation. While suffering wasn't considered inherently evil, it wasn't seen as good either. It acted as a distraction from virtue and a test of one's character. The Stoic philosopher Epictetus succinctly captured this viewpoint when he said, "It's not what happens to you, but how you react to it that matters." This philosophy was famously paraphrased by Jack Sparrow in *The Pirates of the Caribbean* when he said, "The problem is not the problem. The problem is your attitude about the problem."

In contrast, Epicurus, who founded his own school of philosophy, presented a vastly different perspective on suffering, teaching that the goal of life was not only to seek pleasure and avoid pain, but also to practice moderation and avoid overindulgence. It emphasized the acceptance of death and the rejection of fear towards the gods. Overindulgence was seen as a root cause of suffering, and moderation was the antidote. In the Epicurean view, suffering was considered evil, but an evil of one's own making, arising from a lack of moderation and an overemphasis on external pleasures.

While Stoicism and Epicureanism differed in their views on pleasure, pain, and the nature of suffering, both philosophies emphasized the importance of the individual's internal state and their ability to control their reactions to external events. Both schools of thought encouraged individuals to take responsibility for their own happiness and well-being and to cultivate a mindset that would enable them to navigate life's challenges with resilience and equanimity.

Now, some of you reading this are probably quite frustrated with me. I covered Stoicism and then continued on without mentioning Marcus Aurelius. You thought I was going to give a brief summary of Stoicism, mentioning and quoting Jack Sparrow but not the most famous Stoic of all, didn't you? No, that would be crazy. One of the most famous books of all time is his book, or more accurately his diary, *Meditations*. In it he says, "The impediment to action advances action. What stands in the way becomes the way." Arguably, the most famous Stoic of all time took suffering as the path forward, not one of many but the singular path forward. Alas, we begin to see a more nuanced understanding of this once resplendent and intricate word. A word that, like much of the English language, has deteriorated and has been diluted, muted, regressed, and diminished. The word now subsides as a common expression, banal and devoid of meaning.

We cannot forget Eastern thought. No, I didn't forget about "ya'll" like most Westerners do. How could I? Buddha is one of the most often quoted men on earth. In regard to suffering, he may be the most quoted man to have ever lived.

Don't Forget the East

Buddhism is prevalent across the world, when looked at as a philosophy instead of a religion it seeps into practically every orifice of modern understanding and contemplation on the subject. There exist Christians, Muslims, and atheists who subscribe to many of the Buddhist practices. The core of Buddhist practice and philosophy centers on the alleviation of suffering. This is evident in the Four Noble Truths, which diagnose the nature and cause of suffering, and the Eightfold Path, which outlines the way to overcome it. Of course, Buddha himself was far more nuanced than this. Reducing his thoughts to the simple goal of "ending suffering" is a gross oversimplification. I am merely offering a quick and coarse course. An entire book could be written on just the Buddhist understanding of suffering (and many have).

In summary, suffering is a concept deeply ingrained in the human experience, and, thus, has been a subject of contemplation and debate for all of human history. Its complexity cannot be adequately captured within the confines of a single book, especially with a single chapter of a single book. To delve further into the exploration of this subject within the context of this particular work, it is necessary to establish a foundational agreement, a concession if you will: that suffering, generally, is perceived as a negative.

I do not ask or suggest that suffering is inherently evil, or that it should be eradicated. I do not negate the existence of nuanced perspectives that may view suffering as a necessary component of growth, or as a catalyst for transformation. However, for the purposes of this discourse, I ask that you suspend your more critical and contemplative thought for the temporary acceptance of the prevailing modern tendency to view suffering as undesirable and unpleasant.

Chapter 2

Our Stories

"One day, in retrospect, the years of struggle will strike you as the most beautiful."

-Sigmund Freud

We all have those cherished stories that we share whenever we're gathered around a crackling campfire. While one of our friends is adding far more firewood than necessary, poking and prodding at the whisps of flame, we recite our stories. These are stories that our loved ones have heard so many times they could recite them in their sleep, and our closest friends can repeat verbatim, mimicking our inflections and gestures perfectly. These are the tales that have become ingrained in our personal narratives, the experiences that have shaped us and the memories that we hold dear.

A Diving Adventure

One of my many stories begins as a trip I took with our Village's first rescue (mostly recovery) dive team. Our band of volunteer firefighters embarked on an odyssey with an enemy quite the opposite of our usual foe. We had conquered fire and decided to take to task the enemy of our enemy, water. To face such a deadly foe, we needed training. This training would require us to venture from Nebraska to Utah. We were short of funds, and what we did have we spared on equipment. We were determined to conquer the drive in one go, but Mother Nature had other plans. Being in a small Wyoming town a few weeks before Christmas, you can imagine the weather we attempted to ignore. Wyoming winters refuse to be ignored.

The hotels were out of our budget, but so, too, were the tents and sleeping bags. The quaint Wyoming town offered a $50-a-night haven with a temperamental space heater, its warmth a fickle guard against the winter's chill. The heater sputtered and sighed, its ten-minute bursts supplied nothing but a tease. A polite chat with the owner revealed this temperamental heater was the sole source of warmth in the entire establishment, for every other room's heater had completely failed. We did our best to shiver through the night, falling asleep to the symphony of teeth chattering and snores, serving bass was the thump of giving the heater a kickstart. We piled on the blankets and even donned our diving gear until the sun rose in the morning.

The rest of the trip was a resounding success. We passed many of our diving requirements at record rates (or so we were told by our dive master). These included but were not limited to removing, troubleshooting, disassembling, repairing, reassembling, and donning our gear, all at depth. Ascending without our air to simulate running out. Breathing the bubbles from our regulator to simulate a broken regulator or torn hose. We also had the unique opportunity to dive into a near-human temperature hot springs cavern called Homestead Crater. The water within the crater was heated geothermally, creating an environment unlike any other. The sensation of being submerged in this water was truly bizarre; the combination of the water's density and its near-body temperature made it feel almost as if I were floating in extremely humid air. It's challenging to articulate the distinctiveness of both the place itself and the feeling of being suspended within its warm, buoyant waters.

At the Bonneville Sea Base, the water was far less inviting. Hovering at forty degrees, the cold pierced through our suits. The unique salt concentration allowed for all sorts of sea life in the middle of a desert. Practicing our buoyancy control, attempting to gracefully glide amongst the ocean's denizens. However, any vigorous kick or accidental bump into the seabed transformed the once pristine underwater into a chaotic maelstrom of fish feces and discarded scales. An eruption akin to a prairie storm cloud, a cumulonimbus explosion. An underwater blizzard, only instead of snowflakes, we were engulfed in a flurry of fishy debris. The turbidity absorbed our hands and fellow divers, the dimly glowing compass, our only refuge, our only means of escape.

At the same location, in what I can best describe as an abandoned missile silo, we descended into a murky abyss, a submerged cathedral of darkness. The descent felt like a journey to the underworld, faint, ghostly lights marking our passage into the depths at fifteen-foot increments. When we reached the bottom, the world dissolved into a sensory deprivation chamber. Sight was useless; we were blind as bats in a coal cellar. Our hands vanished before our eyes, swallowed by the inky blackness. The telephone game took on a new dimension, a silent symphony of tugs and pulls on a rope. Each tug was a word, each pause a punctuation mark, a conversation conducted in a language only our nerves could understand. The divers' Morse code, but instead of instruction detailed by dits and dahs, clicks and clacks, it was silent tugs.

We were told it was a test of our ability to communicate, a necessary quest to achieve our Altitude Diving and Depth certifications. In reality, it was a test of our mettle, a trial by darkness, where the only way out was through. Keeping your nerves, handling your fears, the ability to stay calm is one of the most crucial survival skills.

I would imagine many of you found the latter half of this story far more enthralling (if at all). Yet, when we reminisce, it is rarely on the beauty of the fish (I can't recall a single one), the lovely temperature and sensation of the crater, or even our achievements. We almost always reminisce on the depth and darkness of the silo, the frigid 40 degree water, or surviving the freezing hotel room. Why do we focus and fixate on the perceivably worse portions of the trip?

A Good Old Fashioned Poor-Off

Growing up with limited means, as I did, fosters a unique camaraderie. There's a bond formed across cultures by the shared experience of squeezing every ounce of joy from the simplest scenarios. You may notice a quirky bit of lighthearted fun that those who grew up in less comfort will participate in regardless of where they come from. I refer to it as a 'poor off'. Where we playfully compete to determine who endured a greater hardship. It isn't about determining who had it worse; it's the communal recognition of those who have been through it and have learned to see the humor.

I am sure you have seen it or even participated in a situation similar to the one below:

"We grew up living off nuffin' but cheese and

bologna sandwiches! That government cheese was wayyy better than the stuff in the yellow box we get today!"

"Cheese? Oh wow, you were living the high life! We only had the bologna, if you could call it that! It was definitely some kinda meat, but not a part of the pig I could recognize!"

"More than just bread and butter? You were sitting pretty high on the hog, weren't you?"

"Wait, butter? You mean margarine, right? Because only the really fancy folks had REAL butter in our day. That stuff was exxxpeeeensive!"

"Mom's handmade bread was the best. I can still taste it. The store-bought stuff? Pfft, we couldn't afford it. That stuff was for the rich and it didn't even taste as good."

"I hated having to go to the Salvation Army to get new pants! They never had my size, and they always felt weird."

"You got new pants? All I got was my brother's hand-me-downs. It didn't even matter if I fit in them yet. He always got mad at me for going in his room to get them because Mom forgot they were mine."

"You had your own room? All the boys in my house shared a room."

"Your brothers let you share a room? I had to sleep in the living room!"

"Wait, you guys had a living room? We had 8 kids in a 2 bedroom house! Only the girls got a bedroom."

While humorous, simple fun, these exchanges are indicative of the truth of our view of suffering, a profound interaction. These little exchanges, where we laugh about our past struggles, show we relish in them after the fact. We don't shy away from them or try to bury them. We romanticize our past struggles, wearing them as badges of honor. They make us who we are. They are who we are. They shape our identity and become an integral part of our personal narrative. They are our little proofs of strength and wisdom. These are our stories and our memories that we carry with us, twisting them into tales of triumph, weaving them into the fabric of who we are.

These real world renderings are far greater tools of revelation than our pointed and scholarly thoughts on the subject, more revealing than anything a textbook or academic paper could ever offer. They are naturally derived, unscripted, organic and unfiltered by the constraints of scholarly analysis, the often forced rigor and proofs associated with academic discourse. There's no formula here, no forced rigor. Just the organic, messy beauty of life as it is, struggles and all.

First Responders

The tendency to glamorize past suffering transcends socioeconomics and manifests as a pervasive aspect of human nature. It's a universal human trait and often isn't as light-hearted as the previous examples. There are the stories we tell around a campfire, and there are the stories we refuse to tell. Yet, we know that going back to the stories we don't want to tell are exactly how we overcome them. The act of revisiting past traumas carries a profound significance. The stories we refuse to share, even with the experienced elders who have endured far greater and numerous hardships, are the exact stories we must tell. Confronting and narrating our most painful experiences is integral to overcoming them. It is as if the stories are living and breathing, demanding to be told. Willing to destroy their own source of life, their author, when their demands are not met.

This paradox lies at the heart of what it is to be human: the experiences that cause us the most profound suffering also hold the keys to our liberation. By refusing to acknowledge and share these experiences, we inadvertently destroy ourselves, but by bravely facing our past and giving voice to our pain, we initiate a process of healing and transformation.

We first responders must tell our tales of 65 mph fiery maelstroms burning across the plains leaving petrified cattle in their wake. The once deafening sounds of the stampede for survival driven silent by the roaring winds, exploding trees, and crackling underbrush. The burning house, a somber picture, framed by a windbreak of cedars that remain miraculously green. Knowing we are in the wrong truck, waves of impotence, total helplessness, praying that everyone escaped.

Turning our backs and charging through the dense smoke and ash. Fire on all sides, a heat so intense it makes you wonder how the paint on the truck refrains from flaking off. The wind is blowing so hard that chunks of trees, still on fire, are blowing overhead as you sit in awe. Then you hear them begin to crash into you. Your total acceptance of defeat, blinded and disoriented, not knowing where to go. Then your brethren appear with their spotlight laden grass rig, heavenly lights, a guiding star leading us out of the gray haze. A literal ray of hope.

Escaping the grey hell only to enter a new level of Dante's imagination, a pitch black pasture lit only by the soft orange glow of the roaring fire. Farmers navigate through the burning hellscape in their plastic covered tractors, fenders melting off as they frantically drag discs through their freshly planted fields all to starve the fire of fuel. The surprisingly powerful weapon they wield to prevent their homes and livelihoods from escaping them as a soft piece of ash floating towards the heavens.

Our stories of the twisted and mutilated corpses. How surprised you were when greeted by a protruding femur as you begin the painstaking process of extracting a man from the wreckage of a car wrapped around a tree. The realization that you weren't surprised by the comfortable heated leather seats turned into a mangled metal prison, nor were you surprised by the man's deafening screams as we tightened the tourniquet. No, at first you were surprised by how dry the bone appeared, not glistening and bloody as you would expect. Much cleaner than you would have imagined. Then you were surprised by the screams; they weren't just screams of pain but his only ability to tell his story. His insistence on being able to tell his story. It wasn't his fault as he exclaimed, "I told them I was too tired to come to work."

In contrast, your surprise with yourself when you saw the brains of a man laying cleanly on the hood of his car. It's not the violent chaos you expected. Al-

Chapter 2: Our Stories

most as if it was sat down gently for later use. Delicately and purposely placed. In that moment, you catch yourself, internally noticing and asking yourself, "how cold is your heart?" As you stop yourself from thinking that this was in fact his fault. This was his painting of his life, the evidence of his decisions, a life he chose to live, leading him down a path that ended with a needle, a rush of addictive euphoria, a life snuffed out in an instant, and ten men cleaning up another one of his messes. It's hard not to feel a sense of inhumanity when you face the reality of what he's left behind. Then your mind snaps back, the realization of your sadistic coping mechanism. How many of us, in the wrong circumstances, might make the same misstep, might be lured by the same promises of escape? Did his parents do anything wrong? Are they going to blame themselves? What is going to happen to them? Are you going to make the same mistake with your children? STOP! It doesn't matter now, you have a job to do. Push those thoughts back and tell the story later.

The last breath of a child as we raced to the hospital, straddling the limits the engine's governor set upon us, an engineer's tool to suffocate the ambulance's sense of urgency. Why would you limit my vessel of safety? I need that extra few miles per hour. The road is barren. Please let me go faster, please! In the front, we maintain our focus, eyes locked on the road, fighting the impulse to look back, to look at the child whose life is slipping through our fingers. Our counterparts in the back, focused and relentlessly performing chest compressions on a darkening blue precious baby, each pump an act of desperate hope. In that moment, you don't think about what's next, you only think about what's slipping away, struggling not to lose this precious chance of what could be lived, not wanting to lose this battle to revive those who left us long before we arrived. The battle is lost and we know it, but we keep fighting. Not because we believe we can win, but because we owe them everything, the chance they never got, the life they'll never know. Every ounce of energy goes into that fight, that desperate attempt to bring them back, to give them even a fraction of the life they should have had.

In the hospital your Captain looks at you knowingly. This is the first child you watched pass. This is a twin, just a few weeks younger than your twins. He puts his hand on your shoulder but doesn't need to ask. You feel it. The cold certainty that, despite your best efforts, you couldn't save them. That you have lost this battle. Then he says the powerful words, "How are you?" In that moment, the tears burn like acid as they sneak down your cheeks. You nod and say, "I'm okay," while being overcome by the sense of how utterly selfish you are for thanking God that isn't your child. You get back, put the ambulance away, and get the opportunity to walk into your children's room and hold them as you cry yourself to sleep. How utterly selfish.

In our rural communities, we face a unique challenge when tragedy strikes, a challenge unlike any other. The kind of tragedy that forces you to witness a person you've watched grow from a toddler to a girl and finally a woman, lying lifeless in a corn field. Her car, a twisted overturned testament to the violence of the crash, lay hidden behind the rows of corn it leaped over. She's barefoot, clothes torn, and half-ripped off, her body a canvas of destruction. Yet, it's not her physical state that overwhelms you, but the eerie calmness that seems to settle over the situation.

It's a numbing stillness, a total acceptance of the tragedy unfolding before you. The training takes control, telling us how exactly to react. Our emotions don't need to be set to the side; it's as if they don't exist. Compartmentalized and subjugated. We are the calm in the storm, the necessary force to act, not feel.

The wails of her family...wait this is your family your Niece and your Sister-in-Law, echo through the field. Standing there, also barefoot, is your niece, with holes reminiscent of bullet wounds from the corn stalks piercing through her muscle, covered in stickers from toe to hip gathered by running to look for help. Your Mother-in-Law staring at you desperately for any chance of hope, any small gesture, any notion from your body language that her precious daughter is alive. A gesture you can't provide.

Yet, you peacefully assess this situation, the adrenaline in your blood calming your trembling hands as you search for a pulse. Knowing you will find no such evidence of life, you know your family will not be so lucky. Just in case, only because that is what your training tells you to do, you refrain from moving her at all. Just as expected, you find no pulse but much to your surprise you hear your name whispered from those fragile lips. Then, the time of day and the names of your children spoken so softly, as if by an angel. As it must be, for there is no way this girl I helped raise is alive. As the other responders flood into the field, she addresses them by name and receives a fervent apology from a girl who cannot move. You realize this is real; it wasn't the whispers of an angel. The drowning sirens are silent in your mind, all your attention is on immobilizing her neck. As you carry her through the ditch on a hard plastic board, joining your niece with a robe of stickers, all your attention is on her neck, for you do not want to be the one that ends this miracle.

When the situation is over and they are safely in the hands of the surgeons. The realization of your callus acceptance, the total inability to feel the pains of loss, wash over you. The adrenaline dumps and your eyes close as the tears fall. The tears do not well because you thought your sister was dead, nor are they tears of joy from realizing she isn't. They form at the realization of how easily you accepted her death. Your training has done its job too well. Your heart had been hardened, made numb by similar calls. You had been forced to accept loss before it even registered in your mind. The tears fall not from sorrow, but from the unsettling truth that, for a brief moment, you had allowed yourself to accept the inevitability of her death without the drop of a tear or the deep-aching, heart-dropping sensation.

These are the stories we share only with those who truly understand. In these shared moments of hardship, we find not just solace, but a deeper connection, a bond forged through the very suffering that others have faced and overcome. Our struggles, regardless of where they come from, transform into the pillars of our strength and resilience. It is not in the moments of comfort that our true selves are revealed; it is in the trials we endure and emerge from that we are defined. We don't simply survive suffering, but we seek it, not for the pain itself, but because it is through that pain that we are shaped.

It's in the stories we share with others, the raw, unvarnished truth of our experiences. No one is drawn to hear of your quiet evenings spent at home, watching TV, or lounging in your yard grilling burgers with a cold beer in hand. What resonates, what captures the heart and mind, are the stories of those rare moments when living itself became harder than dying. It's in the suffering, the struggle, and the overcoming that we find meaning and identity.

This is the paradox, that in death we find our life. In death, we find our strength and our limits. These are not simply stories but narratives. An echo of what the world, dare I say God, wants out of us. It is what others want out of us. It is what society sees in us. It is the value you bring to those with whom you surround yourself. This isn't simply a story, but it is the orientation, the purpose of our lives. It is what we were born to do. The answer to the meaning of life is far better than 42, as Douglas Adams would have it; it is suffering.

Chapter 3

The Effects

"Out of suffering have emerged the strongest souls; the most massive characters are seared with scars."

- Kahlil Gibran

Suffering has been studied intently long before the scientific method was derived by men with a belief in an ultimate truth. Long before the advent of empirical methodologies. Chapter 1 elucidates the ponderings of philosophers and theologians grappling with the nature and implications of suffering but what of the men of measurements? Tangible measurables, the physical realm can be easier and more subjective to interact with. While these early thinkers relied on introspection and reason, the rise of scientific investigation introduced new tools and perspectives for understanding this complex phenomenon. The scientific method, with its emphasis on observation, measurement, and experimentation, offered a seemingly objective approach to studying the subjective experience of suffering. They can be manipulated through poor statistical analysis or begin with an outcome predetermined by the measurer. Damning incongruous data can be referred to as an outlier and ignored for the sake of the narrative. Biases and preconceptions can influence the design and interpretation of research. The selection of data, the choice of statistical analyses, and the framing of conclusions can all be subtly shaped by the researcher's underlying assumptions. Worst of all, our mind and our emotions can be deconstructed to a mere chemical reaction.

Yet, they leave shadows and remnants to be assessed by men from all ages. New data and new tools can shed light or build upon studies performed 100 years prior. In accordance with this modern belief, what does 'the science' offer on a seemingly philosophical endeavor? It offers insights into suffering's role in human development. Subjective interpretations abound, empirical research provides compelling evidence that embracing suffering is not merely an unavoidable reality but a positive force that fosters resilience, meaning, and personal growth—a weapon of our allies not our enemies. The exploration of suffering extends far beyond the confines of modern scientific inquiry.

The Psychological Impact of Suffering

The intricate psychological ramifications of suffering have been extensively explored, yielding profound insights into the human capacity for resilience and growth amidst adversity. Viktor Frankl's seminal work *Man's Search for Meaning* emerged from the depths of the Holocaust. It proved suffering, when imbued with meaning and purpose, is a source of existential fulfillment rather than despair. He observed that Holocaust victims who found purpose in their suffering were significantly more resilient and less likely to succumb to hopelessness. Built upon this is logotherapy, which utilizes the human ability of deriving meaning from suffering to overcome our mind's ailments. It showed that suffering was more an internal decision than an external event.

Contemporary psychological research corroborates this breakthrough notion. Studies on post-traumatic growth posit that individuals who undergo significant adversity often experience profound psychological benefits, including increased appreciation for life, deeper relationships, and greater personal strength. Pioneering researchers such as Richard Tedeschi and Lawrence Calhoun have documented the profound existential awakening and reevaluation of life's priorities that frequently accompany the experience of trauma.

Stress inoculation therapy, along with other behavioral based therapies, has revealed the expected advantage of controlled exposure to moderate stress levels. This exposure has been shown to strengthen an individual's resilience against future challenges. The concept may seem self-evident to many—it aligns with the age-old adage of facing one's fears. However, in the scientific community, empirical evidence is paramount. Hence, research studies were conducted to substantiate this seemingly intuitive notion.

These studies delved into the mechanisms by which moderate stress exposure enhances coping mechanisms. They explored how controlled exposure to stressors can trigger physiological and psychological adaptations that bolster an individual's ability to manage future adversity. The findings underscored the importance of striking a balance between stress avoidance and excessive stress exposure. Utilizing this method, one can slowly increase the stress exposure to higher and higher limits. This method, known as systematic desensitization, allows individuals to adapt and build resilience, expanding their comfort zone and ultimately increasing their stress tolerance threshold. Through repeated and controlled exposure, individuals can learn to manage and cope with increasingly challenging situations, thereby mitigating the negative impacts of stress and enhancing their overall well-being. Thus, enforcing the paradox of the disease also being the medicine.

Mark Seery and colleagues showed that moderate adversity leads to the highest reported life satisfaction and lowest distress levels. Their analysis was visually represented by a distinctive curve, where those who have encountered the most adversity paradoxically exhibit greater life satisfaction and lower distress than those who have encountered the least. This paradoxical discovery highlights the crucial role that suffering plays in cultivating psychological resilience, well-being, and life satisfaction. More importantly, it suggests that suffering is not merely a byproduct of life but a necessary component for achieving a fulfilling and meaningful existence. In the absence of suffering, it should be sought. In the pursuit of happiness (whatever that means), one must also pursue suffering. The paradox knows no bounds. The disease is not only the medicine, but it also shows us again that suffering is what brings life satisfaction. It is not only the antidote to complacency, but also the source of profound meaning and satisfaction. The absence of suffering can lead to a life devoid of purpose and genuine fulfillment.

The Neurological Correlates of Endurance

Neuroscientific research further substantiates the positive power of suffering and has provided sufficient evidence to confirm that experiences of adversity do facilitate positive cognitive adaptations. Brain imaging studies, expressly those utilizing functional

MRI, have revealed heightened activity in the prefrontal cortex of individuals who have endured adversity. This region's functionality is diverse but is critical for complex cognitive processes such as problem-solving, trouble-shooting, emotional regulation, decision-making, strategizing, and long-term planning. The observed increase in neural activity suggests that the experience of suffering strengthens and refines these cognitive functions, thereby enhancing an individual's capacity to navigate future challenges. Thus, there is an increasing likelihood of willfully enduring similar distressing external stimuli and leading to more overall success as measured by modern and evolutionary standards.

The prefrontal cortex is integral to the executive functions, which are higher-order cognitive processes that enable individuals to regulate their thoughts, feelings, and actions to achieve their goals. These include but are not limited to:

- ❖ Working Memory or the ability to hold and manipulate information in mind for short periods. Similar to RAM on a computer, this is crucial for day-to-day problem solving. For example, from maintaining a database of numbers when working on complex equations in your head to maintaining a database of numbers necessary to dial the telephone of a new customer.

- ❖ Cognitive Flexibility or the ability to switch between different tasks or perspectives. This alone is an extremely crucial skill of any high-level career. This regulates one's ability to handle a stream of focal redirects that persist in any demanding role. To handle an email, upset employee, and phone call simultaneously. It is also crucial for dispute resolution, the ability to view perspectives of others and articulate that position to others.

- ❖ Inhibitory Control or the ability to suppress thoughts or actions, regardless of their nature, including delayed gratification. This is exemplified by the Stanford marshmallow experiment. This deliciously iconic study revealed that resisting the siren call of a single marshmallow demonstrated one's ability to endure short-term discomfort in pursuit of long-term rewards. This most fluffy test showed a human's capacity to delay gratification directly correlated with overall discipline and strategic thinking—strong predictors of success in various life domains.

- ❖ Emotional Regulation, which is crucial for maintaining and improving mental health as well as fostering healthy relationships. Superior emotional regulation skills benefit you in every facet of life, from marriage and caring for children to management and accounting. Patience, a key indicator of emotional regulation, is necessary for any level of conflict resolution, education, training, or teaching.

The more advanced one's executive functions, the better they perform in all domains, including academic achievement, professional advancement, life satisfaction, intimate and non-intimate relationships, and emotional well-being.

Overall, the research suggests that the experience of suffering will catalyze positive cognitive and emotional adaptations, quite literally rewiring and restructuring the human brain in a manner that enhances the individual's ability to cope with and overcome future challenges. While undeniably difficult and painful, suffering is the mechanism for growth and development of the human mind. By learning to manage their emotions, cultivate resilience, and think strategically, individuals who have experienced adversity can emerge from their struggles with newfound strength and capability.

The Sociocultural Benefits of Collective Struggle

Suffering is not merely an individual experience; it is a fundamental aspect of social cohesion. Historical analysis reveals that societies that endure collective hardship, such as war, famine, or economic depression, often emerge with stronger cultural identities and more robust ethical frameworks. The shared hardship fosters a sense of solidarity and mutual support, leading to the strengthening of social bonds and an overall more robust culture willing to work together and see from one another's perspective than to join arms against each other.

The adversity faced by the Greatest Generation exemplifies the transformative power of collective suffering. Surviving the Great Depression, the Dust Bowl, and World War II instilled a sense of duty, resilience, and communal solidarity that profoundly shaped the moral fabric of the early 20th century. Emphasizing values such as self-sacrifice, service, and the importance of the collective good. The economic hardship and deprivation of the Depression instilled a sense of resilience and resourcefulness. The Dust Bowl formed integrated communal relationships of dependence, breaking through racial and nationalistic divides, turning nemeses into neighbors while the war effort fostered a sense of duty, patriotism, and communal solidarity.

Anthropological research on rites of passage further illustrates the social utility of suffering. Male organizations still practice this today, but it was common in almost all indigenous cultures. Initiation rituals involving physical pain or endurance serve as transformative experiences that mark the transition from adolescence to adulthood. These rituals reinforce communal bonds and instill a profound sense of identity and belonging, demonstrating that suffering can serve as a conduit for personal and collective transformation.

I am no soldier and can only speak from what I see, but the shared experience of knowing the same suffering fosters a strong sense of community, group identity, belonging, and solidarity among initiates. It creates a bond forged in hardship. The individual, through suffering, is integrated into the collective, their personal identity intertwined with the social fabric of the community. They will run into a wall of bullets for one another, scale a cliff to carry a dying brother down, crawl through the mud made of blood not water—they will not leave each other behind. That bond is only formed by men of the same forge, the same blacksmith, and the same hammer.

The endurance of suffering is seen as proof of character and resilience, qualities necessary in these societies. Successfully navigating the trials of initiation builds trust and demonstrates the individual's ability to withstand hardship. Proving not only their worthiness to assume the responsibilities of adulthood, but also their ability to respond in adulthood. Allowing for those who will be reliant on them to feel secure in being reliant on them. A process of proving oneself through suffering is a form of social selection, ensuring that only those deemed capable are granted full membership in the community for the sake of the community.

Prior to entering these rituals, the men may not be prepared or willing. Choice, a modern taken-for-granted luxury. We live in a world where only the willing sign up for war. Only those who enjoy the challenge hunt. For most of human history, it was a duty for the sake of those around them. It was their means of food. Their means of safety. The experience of suffering prepared them, heightened their sense of self-awareness, self-confidence, courage, and defined their place in society. A sense of worth not available otherwise. The physical and emotional challenges faced during initiation pushes individuals to their limits, forcing them to confront their fears and weaknesses. This process of self-confrontation forms them into what society needs out of them and what they need out of themselves.

The Paradox of Comfort

If suffering is integral to growth, then its avoidance must cause withering deformation. In insulating ourselves from hardship, we do not preserve strength; we atrophy. Contemporary Western societies, increasingly buffered from the raw edges of existence, show rising levels of anxiety, depression, and a persistent sense of meaninglessness. It is no coincidence. These afflictions do not arise in spite of comfort but because of it.

Postmodernism, in its rejection of grand narratives, truth, and meaning has dismantled traditional structures that once held suffering in a redemptive light. What remains is a culture engaged in ontological and epistemological crises, yearning for significance in curated identities and micro-traumas. In the absence of real suffering, hunger, war, loss, grief, they seek its shadow in the form of perceived offenses and systemic victimhood. It is not a cry for justice, but a hunger for purpose and identity.

Jonathan Haidt and Greg Lukianoff's concept of "safetyism," as explored in *The Coddling of the American Mind*, reveals how shielding young people from adversity results not in stronger individuals, but in psychological brittleness. When children are raised under the dogma that discomfort is harm and disagreement is danger, they do not grow resilient. They grow afraid and weak. They enter adulthood with the emotional immune systems of infants, unable to metabolize pain, opposition, or contradiction.

Thus, in a culture obsessed with avoiding suffering, suffering mutates, it adapts to stay relevant. It no longer shapes but haunts. It no longer purifies but paralyzes. We are left with the consequences of a society that has forgotten a brutal truth: Suffering is not the enemy. Comfort is.

Furthermore, the phenomenon of hedonic adaptation, our innate tendency to return to a psychological baseline after both triumph and tragedy, reveals the futility of a life built around comfort. No matter how lavish, secure, or curated one's environment becomes, the emotional high fades. The pleasure that once thrilled becomes the new norm. The goalposts of happiness shift, always out of reach. Thus, the pursuit of perpetual comfort is not only cowardly…it is self-defeating.

Affective neuroscience confirms what ancient wisdom has always known: the path to enduring fulfillment does not lie in the avoidance of pain, but in its confrontation. Those who chase pleasure find themselves dulled, desensitized, dependent. But those who endure hardship, who face the storm rather than flee from it, develop resilience, meaning, and depth.

We are not wired for endless comfort. We are wired for overcoming. And when that fundamental reality is denied, when we anesthetize every ache, cancel every offense, sanitize every environment, we do not thrive. We disintegrate.

Suffering as a Prerequisite for Fulfillment

The empirical evidence overwhelmingly supports the proposition that suffering, far from being an evil to be eradicated, is a fundamental aspect of human flourishing. It refines character, fosters resilience, enhances cognitive abilities, strengthens social cohesion, and imbues life with profound meaning. To reject suffering is to reject the very mechanism through which individuals and societies evolve.

Thus, the choice before us is not whether we will suffer, but how we will engage with life when a chance for living arrives. Those who embrace suffering as a transformative force unlock its potential to cultivate wisdom, endurance, and existential depth.

Those who flee from it, seeking refuge in comfort, risk stagnation and disillusionment. As the Stoic philosopher Seneca wrote, "Difficulties strengthen the mind, as labor does the body." The acceptance of suffering is not an act of resignation but an affirmation of life's most profound truths. It is the act of living.

This perspective challenges the notion that suffering is solely a negative force to be avoided or eradicated. Instead, it suggests that suffering isn't simply harnessed as a tool for self-development and spiritual growth, but it also exists as the sole tool. While the subjective nature of suffering makes it difficult to study definitively, the weight of scientific evidence points towards it being as necessary a component of human development as fire is to a forge just as integral to life as food and water.

In essence, the scientific exploration of suffering reveals the paradox: while it is an experience often associated with pain, loss, and despair, it is the means for overcoming pain, loss, and despair. It is the disease and the medicine. This paradoxical nature of suffering highlights the complexity of the human languages or lack thereof. It displays our contradictory understanding of suffering.

Out of Studies into Stories

All of this is known intuitively, but also upon societal inspection of our stories. Yes, we see it in statistics and charts, but more so in the most honest mirrors we have, the faces of our children.

Children of the ultra-wealthy are adorned in designer clothes and surrounded by endless toys, but they live in a strange silence. Their world is filled with 'things'. They have castles made of plastic and closets overflowing with clothes, more shoes than a family of five could wear in a year, more video game worlds than one could explore in a lifetime. Yet, there is a vacancy behind their eyes, a certain hunger that the mountain of junk food and candy in their marble kitchen cannot satisfy. Their joy is often fleeting, short-circuited and interrupted by endless novelty, overstimulation, and the hollow echo of "yes."

Contrast this with children of poverty. The child with one pair of shoes with a pinky toe sticking out, a cracked toy truck that barely survived their older brother, and a stick from an old hickory tree that magically becomes a sword, a flying broom, a horse, and a lightning staff to conquer all kingdoms. There is a level of stress that the child has endured, no doubt. Hunger, uncertainty, danger. But when joy breaks through in such a life, it is radiant. When that child smiles, the world holds its breath. The light in his eyes is not manufactured; rather, it is forged. It is real.

The poor child's story is the one we want to hear. Not because we are voyeurs of pain, but because it speaks to something older, something true. We see grit, creativity, tenacity. We see someone who has learned to make beauty from scarcity. A child who laughs not because life has given him every reason to, but because he has decided to. That smile, against all odds, resembles the stars. Brilliant, distant, and impossible to extinguish.

The wealthy child may inherit fortune, but the impoverished child inherits character. The stories of the rich often end in collapse. White-walled rehab clinics, grey-walled prisons, brown-walled coffins, or hollow mansions echoing with the sound of loneliness. No one writes fairy tales about yachts and trust funds. The story of the boy who shared a single bowl of rice with his siblings, the girl who stitched her own dress from scraps, the kids who built kingdoms from cardboard, these are the stories that fill our books, our screens, and our dreams.

Their stories are written onto the parchment of choice in every culture, in every tongue. They are legends and heroes, not because they were comfortable, but because they suffered, and in doing so, became something the world needed. Something holy and respected, nay loved.

This is not a glorification of poverty. This is not a romantic lie about how suffering is sweet and secretly fun. Suffering is not sweet—it is bitter, violent, and cold. Exactly the way we like it. When endured, when met with spirit rather than resentment, it births something eternal. The child wins because he was poor, not despite it. He wins because he found meaning in the midst of what should have broken him. He wins not because he imagined something better, but because he knew there could be worse. He chose to live as the world is, one smile at a time.

What did comfort give the wealthy child? What does comfort truly give us….more importantly, what does it take away?

Chapter 4

Transcendentals

"The world promises you comfort, but you were not made for comfort. You were made for greatness."

- Pope Benedict XVI

In a life of anguish, how do we define what is truly good? What guides us towards the ultimate truth? Where does beauty transcend the boundaries of subjective interpretation? These are the profound questions that have long troubled humanity, leading to a paradox that challenges our understanding of the divine.

Can that which directs us towards God be inherently evil? If so, does this not cast a shadow upon the very nature of God, making him inherently evil? This is the central dilemma that I grappled with. Goodness, Truth, and Beauty are the transcendentals that orientate our aim towards that which lies beyond the limitations of our earthly existence. If suffering orients us toward the almighty and suffering is evil, then is it not an evil almighty? Does it not raise questions about the nature of that divine entity?

Goodness, Truth, and Beauty are the three commonly accepted transcendentals. They incline us to reach out past our grasp, striving for that which is greater than ourselves and always out of reach. They orientate us towards our ultimate goal, an achievement that lies beyond our individual capabilities. They are intertwined in such a manner that they cannot be separated. Why these three?

The paradox of suffering and its ability to guide us towards the divine raise profound questions about the nature of God. It challenges us to reconcile the existence of evil with the concept of a benevolent and omnipotent deity.

Goodness

Though Goodness is rarely listed first among the transcendentals, I begin with it here because it is the most complex and perhaps the most misunderstood.

It is a concept drenched in religious and philosophical tradition. To understand Truth and Beauty, one must begin by grappling with Goodness. To understand Truth and Beauty, one must understand what Goodness is.

What is good for the goose is good for the gander. Birds of a feather have similar beliefs on what good entails. Birds of different kinds may stand in opposition—what is good for you may not be good for me. What is good for the Hawk may not be good for the dove. If we have different moral perspectives, we may disagree on what good actions are. This complexity leads to the oversimplification of goodness, often dismissed as subjective. I must satisfactorily quench that argument before I am able to proceed. A bold and difficult endeavor, for the greatest minds only abstractly agreed on what goodness is:

> "The Good, then, is what gives truth to the things known and the power to know the knower."
>
> Plato's *Republic*, Book VI, 508e

Plato identifies the Good as the highest form, what many today would call God. It is beyond being; it is being. It is the source of reality and knowledge. Goodness is akin to the sun where without the Sun, vision and existence in itself wouldn't be possible in our solar system. In fact, it wouldn't be a solar system at all. For Plato, to know the Good is to know the purpose and essence of all things.

"The good is that at which all things aim."

Aristotle's *Nicomachean Ethics*, Book I, 1094a

Aristotle takes a teleological approach or a purpose rather than cause approach, everything has an end (telos), and the good is that fulfillment. For humans, the highest good is eudaimonia, a Greek idea often translated as "flourishing" or "blessedness" through virtue. His idea would be akin to Goodness is the purpose of our actions, and the results of our actions determine their goodness. For instance, if a car gets you to work, then that is a good car because its purpose is to get you to work. A Rolls-Royce that does not run is not a good car because it does not

Chapter 4: Transcendentals

achieve its purpose. A billionaire who donates a million dollars to charity for a tax write-off is not performing a good act because the purpose of charity is to help others, not gain yourself a tax write-off. Regardless of the outcome, the telos of charity is distorted by the Billionaire.

> "For when the will abandons what is above itself, and turns to what is lower, it becomes evil not because that to which it turns is evil, but because the turning itself is wicked."
>
> Augustine's *City of God*, Book XII, ch. 6

Augustine defines goodness as proper order. Everything is good when oriented toward God. Evil arises not from created things, but from the will's disordered love turning away from the highest Good. The act is not what makes it evil, but the disregard of the orientation is what makes it evil. If one believes they are acting in the proper orientation, then it is not evil (though it is still wrong). If the orientation is correct but the results are evil, then that act is still good (also still wrong). If a knife was built correctly but is used as a spoon, then that is a bad act. If a knife is used to perform surgery, but the surgery fails or by accident harms another part of the body by cutting too deep. The act is good.

> "Goodness and being are really the same, and differ only in idea... For everything is good so far as it is desirable."

Thomas Aquinas's *Summa Theologiae*, I, q. 5, a. 1

Aquinas marries Aristotle's and Augustine's thoughts. All that exists is good because it participates in Being (God), and the good is simply being. Evil does not exist because it is simply the privation of good. Just as light exists and dark does not exist, darkness is the absence of that which does exist, in this case light. Evil is the act that exists without Goodness. You can't see evil; you can only see the absence of Goodness. Anything that acts contrary to being is then an act that moves away from Goodness.

These definitions, though extremely thought-provoking and meaningful, are still relatively ambiguous and potentially subjective. They lack a certain pragmatism or efficaciousness that I desire in this writing. Thus, with much humility, I ask for the use of this definition that attempts to align all these prior definitions in a more subjective manner:

Goodness is the degree to which one aligns with its nature.

Consider a knife. Its nature is to cut. When it cuts, it is good, not because we like the result, but because it fulfills its essence. Regardless of how you determine the nature of the object, correctly or incorrectly, its conformity to that nature is good. We can be incorrect in what our nature is, but we can be good if we align with that nature. If we believe a knife is a spoon and design such a knife, then its ability to perform the actions shows its goodness. A knife designed for the purpose of cutting may not be a good knife to you. This may seem subjective, for it is us, the user, who determine goodness.

This example shows that it takes a being on intellect and reason to determine an object's nature. Only beings with reason can assign purpose. A dog sees a stick; we see a tool, a sword, a flying broom, a horse, and a lightning staff to conquer all kingdoms. Goodness begins not in the object, but in the being who discerns its telos. A dog cannot determine an object's nature. Thus, an object not being perceived or acted upon by a being of intellect cannot be good or bad. A stick in the woods is simply a stick. The goodness transcends the object and focuses on the user. It points us higher than the object.

This is where Goodness aligns with Truth in such a manner that they cannot be removed from one another, why they are inextricably linked as transcendentals. The knife example probably made you scoff, it sounded absurd…because it is absurd. Though goodness seems subjective, it only appears so because our interpretation is based on intent without consideration of the true nature of the object. The objective true nature still governs the outcome. Goodness cannot reach perfection without truth but exists merely as a means to act and a catalyst for future necessary 'good' actions.

Perfect attempted acts of goodness, when fraught with falsehoods, can destroy. The idiom, "the road to hell is paved with good intentions," captures the essence of the results of goodness without truth. We are finite beings with infinite points of necessary knowledge to act. We being finite cannot grasp the infinite pieces of information necessary to act truly good, but we must try, and we can only try when we combine the transcendentals. To refer back to the simpler example of the knife, without truth there will be many mouths cut and bowls of porridge spilled because those who believe that a knife is a spoon are simply wrong. They have focused on the good and neglected truth.

Goodness relates to beauty in much the same manner, both are grounded not in appearance or outcome alone, but in alignment with purpose. In a more lighthearted manner, consider our child's drawing of a horse. If one cannot tell it is a horse, the drawing is not good, in the sense of fulfilling its intended nature, but it is not evil either. It simply lacks the form necessary to be called good. Thus, illustrating Aquinas's thoughts on the subject, evil is not a thing itself but the absence or privation of good. The drawing fails to express what it aims for, thus goodness is absent, not replaced by evil but distorted by misalignment. Can it still be beautiful, unlikely but possible because beauty reflects what is true and good.

A depiction of the sun as a blackhole, cold, devouring, and lightless. If the goal is to accurately depict the sun as it is in our sky, the image fails, it is not good. If the intent is to depict a world in which the light resonates from those that give the sun its purpose, that is life on earth, then this is very good and profoundly beautiful. The sun only has meaning because of what it serves; without the life it nourishes, it is just a ball of fire. In this, beauty emerges not from realism, but from transcendent alignment with a greater truth. Beauty, like Goodness, points beyond itself. We do not judge it rightly unless we understand what it seeks to express.

Just as Goodness requires orientation toward proper ends, Beauty requires purpose, and both demand Truth to be fully known. Without Truth, Goodness can mislead, and Beauty can deceive. A thing cannot be called good if its aim is based on a lie, and it cannot be called beautiful if it reflects a distortion of what is real. Truth is the light by which both Goodness and Beauty are seen for what they are. We cannot know the good or the beautiful unless we first know what the thing is, what it was made for, and whether what we see corresponds to what truly is.

Truth

Truth, like Goodness and Beauty, is not a tool we wield but a reality we uncover gradually, incompletely, and painfully. Truth is always partial, filtered, and distorted, it is obscured by our tools, biases, perspective, history, orientation, intelligence, emotions, etc. It is the goal, the reason we have the scientific method, why philosophy persists, and why theology never ceases. Truth is the foundation of modern science as a whole. If we lack an ultimate truth, then science is a waste of energy, conversation is merely the exchange of personalized falsehoods, and our endeavors are selfish, meaningless acts of power projection.

The post-modernists would have you accept there is no truth, that it never existed. That there is no absolute, only interpretation. A nihilistic selfish existence of power dynamics. We intuitively know this simply isn't true. We know that reality resists our opinions. We measure that which is within our ability to measure, and we have many others do the same in their own manner. When our findings align with the measurements of others, we perceive something real, something True beyond ourselves. It is through these convergences that we confirm the existence of a Truth beyond perspective.

Searching for this truth will eventually lead you to that which is greater than you. The discoveries made bring us closer and closer to that which one could refer to as heaven, God, the almighty, or the universe. Regardless of name, it is infinite, and we are finite. It is before us and after us. It is the shape of all things rightly ordered. It is True whether or not we can ever fully know it. Our finitude cannot extinguish its existence. It is our goal. It is transcendental.

Truth relates deeply to Beauty. That which is not true is often ugly, often in obvious ways but sometimes subtly. We can perceive when something is off in an image, a statement, or a story, even when we cannot articulate why. Consider AI-generated images: a hand with too many fingers, an eye that stares nowhere, a shadow cast at the wrong angle in relation to the light. The discomfort we feel isn't just aesthetic, it's ontological. It is the ugliness of falsehood. Beauty demands Truth because deception is disorder, and disorder is a lie.

Even in art, we encounter this convergence. A depiction of war, though filled with horror, can be beautiful when the image captures the Truth of war. It reveals the horrible unimaginable ways humans truly treat and often see each other. In that revelation, we find meaning.

Mathematics, numbers on a page, are stunningly beautiful as they reveal their order to us. When the Fibonacci sequence and golden ratio were discovered, they were magnificently beautiful. These are not just formulas, but revelations. The symmetry of a snowflake, the spiral of a shell—their beauty lies not only in their appearance, but also in their adherence to an unseen, consistent order. We call them beautiful because they are mathematically true. And when we uncover their purpose, when we see their nature unfold, the beauty deepens.

Truth can be isolated from Goodness and Beauty, but it leaves a terrible stain. It becomes a sterile fact, or a mere observation. Truth without Beauty is clinical and cold, but Truth without Goodness is… brutal. A weapon of precision and no mercy.

In contrast, Truth is the spine upon which Beauty and Goodness are strung. Beauty or Goodness without truth are arguably unimaginable and impossible. Beauty without Truth is deception, a complete illusion, only happening by coincidence or accident. Goodness becomes indulgent and destructive. The villain of most modern Superhero movies, leaving a destructive swath of noble intent.

Beauty

Beauty is harmony, wholeness, clarity. Beauty is recognized because it reflects both truth and goodness. We can recognize the beauty of a seashell, regardless of whether we are particularly fond of calcium coils. A seashell follows a logarithmic spiral much like the golden ratio, and we find this visually appealing. This is partly because it is an efficient growth pattern, good because it allows the snail to flourish with minimal waste. Its telos is achieved as efficiently and efficaciously as possible. A sunflower's perfect arrangement of seeds is not only mathematically precise, but good because it achieves maximum harvest or proliferation at minimum cost. A tree's branching pattern, a river's path, even the fractals etched into the veins of a leaf, each reflects a profound order, where form and function are inseparably married.

Beauty, then, is the outward reflection of inner order: being what it is meant to be, achieving its purpose with wholeness, clarity, and efficiency. Truth reveals, Goodness responds, and Beauty captures that fulfillment in a way the soul instinctively recognizes; not through calculation, but through wonder. We do not reason our way to beauty (though we can); we behold it, and in the beholding, we assent to it.

This recognition is not arbitrary. It is woven into the very fabric of our being. We are drawn to certain wavelengths, certain proportions, certain symmetries across cultures and times because they resonate with the structure of reality itself. What is beautiful is rightly ordered to its nature and rightly ordered to its end, regardless of whether we consciously understand or see these intricacies.

Even decay reveals this truth. When beauty collapses, symmetry fails, or proportions fracture, we feel it as ugliness or discomfort. This is not a random reaction but a universal protest against disorder, against failing to be what it is meant to be. These disorders are signs of disease, rot, and afflictions that we would rather the world lack.

Suffering

These artistic renderings are forms of suffering. They are depictions of what ought to be and what is. In that captured moment, you are not simply capturing an arrangement of photons acting on an arrangement of atoms. You are capturing a metaphysical play, the emotions of the depicted character, the psychological and physiological effects of the state of being, and, most importantly, the emotions of the unseen author, the finite author, and the infinite author—the author working on his canvas of choice and the author of existence.

Now, some of you disagree with me at the moment. You are pointing to a beautiful depiction of a calm, peaceful countryside hanging on your wall. A beautiful scene of the Scottish countryside or a Colorado mountain view cannot be a depiction of suffering? What if it acts as a mirror for the suffering to gaze upon themselves? Where the image is not of a suffering being, but shows the suffering being where they belong and what they are lacking. You are the suffering being, and you are removed from where you belong. It draws a stark contrast to your experience, the grey and black concrete edifices that envelope your daily view. We seek that countryside knowing we can't have it. It is in the act of suffering that we find beauty. Without suffering, we would find these pictures dull and boring. A person who lives in the countryside doesn't need pictures of it.

Suffering is not one of the classical transcendentals, but perhaps it is their footprint or shadow on earth. The mark they leave on the soul as it tries to reach what is beyond. It is the human experience of transcendence failing to manifest completely in time and space. Suffering is what happens when the soul attempts to give birth to the eternal in the temporal. When man reaches for Truth, he suffers falsehood. When he reaches for Goodness, he suffers evil. When he reaches for Beauty, he suffers ugliness.

The very reaching is suffering but the reaching is also what makes him most human and most divine. It is what it means to be alive. To avoid suffering is to live in a numb, ugly, and evil falsehood. To embrace suffering is to aim towards heaven when you know you can't reach it. It is to want the best even when the best is unattainable. It is to reject our fallen nature and strive for our ascended nature. It is to become the best version of ourselves the universe can muster.

Chapter 5

The Paradox and its Elimination

"To love is to suffer. To avoid suffering one must not love. But then one suffers from not loving."

- Woody Allen

All of this is to say that we have built suffering into a paradox, a dilemma. As chapter 1 established, the colloquial use of suffering in the modern English world is one synonymous with pain, anguish, or general living through hardship. It is a catch all for describing life's situations we would rather not experience.

Yet, in chapter 2 we have displayed our nostalgic view of suffering. Our stories of bygone ages and our confrontation with inevitable tragedies. The media we consume in a range of formats tell the stories of others enduring these epics of trial. The living, breathing stories who refuse to be contained even at the expense of their author.

Chapter 3 shows us the results of facing these journeys, life's side missions and quests. The benefits of turning your back on the security of the devil you know for the devil you don't. The benefits, mentally and physically, from enduring and telling these stories.

Chapter 4 established the transcending power of suffering. The essence of God we face when we suffer. The shadow the transcendentals, married or divorced, cast upon us when we experience suffering.

We have sufficiently captured the essence of the paradox. We have hashed the questions: Is suffering an evil, the weapon of our enemy, or is it a good, the shield of our allies? Can it be both good and evil? Does this violate the law on non-contradiction? If an idea cannot be true while simultaneously being false in the same respect, at the same time, can it be evil while simultaneously being good. That which orientates us toward good cannot be in itself evil. Even if we do not enjoy the shove, that shove is an act of good. If the conceptualization and the conception are both good, the anguish that lies between cannot be evil. It is simply necessary.

Where does this leave us? Have we answered the paradox? Can you answer a paradox? Maybe we are asking the wrong question? Maybe in our desire for control and security we have narrowed our perspective? In our arrogant belief that we are the masters of the universe, existing as our own gods capable of understanding the intricacies of a universe that is more vast than our minds can conceptualize and containing corners we will never be able to conquer, we have proposed a definition that comforts our hearts instead of facing our fears. We call suffering both a curse and a crown because our definition is broken.

Death of Definitions

We have, for a time, lost the beauty of language. We have taken for granted the effort of its birth. We have embarked into a world of nonsense, where words are fluid and hold no true meaning. Their use is simply symbolic and evolves with time. In this world, men can be women and moms are birth givers. Square circles exist, if you so wish, and an octagon is an 8-sided square for fear of being racist. We all know this cannot continue, so we stood aside, expecting the herds to grow out of their childish minds as our toddlers learned to walk. As we see this ideology fall apart and the demand for meaning arises, this new edict will give us a rare opportunity for fine tuning our definitions.

The current established definition of suffering via Oxford Language is the state of undergoing pain, distress, or hardship. This is meaningless, much like many words today. If suffering is merely experiencing hardship, then everyone is suffering. We justify these wasted noises fabricated through exhalation and muscle contractions by saying they exist on a "spectrum". The cop out of the simple-minded. This is a waste of breath. If mere existence is on some spectrum of suffering, then suffering itself is meaningless. It's not evil or good; it's nothing. The word serves no purpose other than self-gratification or justification. Words must have meaning; it is intrinsic to their being—the archaic history of their birth. Words are important, and they were born through great effort.

Chapter 5: The Paradox and its Elimination

We already have a word for existing with difficulties. It is Living. We know this intrinsically and we utilize it as such. Would you rather sit at the campfire with those who endured World War One, the depression, then World War Two, or sit alongside those who simply existed. They were living more comfortably than humans have ever lived. Yet, what story do they have to tell? How interesting are their biographies? We know these people have not lived; they have existed. We intrinsically know this. The man going to work, clocking in, clocking out, going to bed, dying naked on the couch eating Cheetos is existing, but is not living.

The greatest man to have ever lived is a man of suffering. A man of stories is a man who has lived, and a man of stories has experienced it all. Yes, he has climbed the greatest mountains, but he lost friends along the way. Yes, he survived the war, but is that easier than being buried in Arlington? Death is not suffering; it is the end of living. It is far easier than surviving. The consequences are unknown, but the result is well-established.

Suffering isn't the only word that has lost its meaning. The word awesome and responsibility, for instance, have been degraded to common use. Awesome being of the same source as awful, but polar opposite in meaning. Awesome couples are God fearing. This is so incredibly powerful that it inspires the utmost respect. It's not a cool skateboard trick but a giant among men, a dragon amongst lizards. It is literally the sights and experiences that man cannot recreate. The thunderstorms of the Midwest prairie, the hurricanes off the Gulf, and the earthquakes in southern California are awesome—your backflip is not. The question from atheists as to why you would fear a loving benevolent God comes from the loss of our ability to convey such a truly awe-inspiring power. It is a question ignorant of time, history, and philology, but is a question that perfectly depicts our piece of time, history, and philology.

Responsibility, the ability to respond, has been utilized as something that is under your management, but it is far more—it is your duty from your God-given ability. A responsibility isn't a choice; rather, it's a gift or a curse that you can choose to ignore at the peril of those around you. The shirking of your responsibility has been degraded to your not doing your job, being lax or lazy. It should be denounced as a neglection of your duty and a loss of your honor. Regardless of your job title, pay scale, or relationship, if you are the most able to respond then this endeavor is your responsibility.

Passion—have you ever wondered why Mel Gibson's movie is called *The Passion of Christ*? Passion means to suffer greatly for. You do not have a passion for the arts unless you have suffered for them. You do not have a passion for Taco Bell or McDonalds. You cannot rightly say that you have a passion until you have given all that there is to give. Yet, today it is simply used as an expression of endearment. A description of an activity you enjoy.

In returning to a world, where names hold power and words hold deep meanings, an endeavor we must embark on, we must ask that these sophisticated philosophical understandings take a role in our proposed definitions. I ask that we eliminate this paradox, that we find a common understanding of the word suffering that doesn't negate the stories we tell and the studies we have performed for the sake of our long-held use of the word. This paradox involves our ontological and epistemological understanding of our surroundings. It will involve a level of harshness. Defining these simple words will require that we stand against the emotions of many who refuse to think with their mind instead of their emotions.

Can a man bear a child?

We should treat this question as the nonsense it is. We should answer adults as we would children. Can a gazelle suffer like a human? Can a tree suffer like a human?

These questions should be equally laughable. The loving and emotional side of us wants to see the world as a tree or a gazelle. To limit the suffering of other beings. Beings that cannot suffer like humans need not requiesce from it. While it is a noble cause, it is a futile endeavor. Merely asking this question reveals who we are and what separates us from animals. It is that very orientation toward the divine, wanting heaven on earth.

What definition could exist to simultaneously remove this paradox, defeat the problem of evil, and degrade a gazelle's or a tree's suffering (or lack thereof)? To bring into congruence Hedonists and Christians, Stoicism and Epicureanism? I propose a new definition:

Chapter 5: The Paradox and its Elimination

Suffering: The uniquely human capacity to consciously compare one's present condition with an imagined ideal.

Can a gazelle suffer if it cannot perceive a situation more favorable than the one it is currently in? Of course not.

Can the lobster in the boiling pot imagine the cool waters of the Northern Atlantic as the fire beneath turns his bath bubbly? No.

Is a dying child, accepting of their fate, suffering? No.

Is a grown man, slowly and painfully dying of cancer, relishing in his opportunity to bring his family together again suffering? Quite the contrary.

Is a mother, holding her child for the last time, calm in her belief he is entering the arms of God for all of eternity, suffering?

Then who is suffering?

The videographer imagines the plains full of gazelle eating safely.

The vegan, yearning for a world where the lobster swims free.

The child who is not ready to go, imagining a world of fishing on the dock and swimming in the pond.

The old man, alone at his bedside, imagining what he could have done differently, a world where he told his children he loved them and he put the cigarettes down and picked up his grandchildren.

The mother whose only belief is that her beloved child will be gone forever, seeking for deeper meaning to this loss or a world where it doesn't exist.

Suffering is not merely hardship, nor is it synonymous with pain. It is the uniquely human act of imagining a reality better than the one currently experienced. It is the ache of knowing what could be and yet is not. A gazelle does not suffer when eaten by a lion but flees instinctively, dies instinctively, and does not mourn its own passing. A lobster in a boiling pot cannot envision the cold depths of the sea, but man can. Man suffers not because he hurts, but because he hopes. He dreams of a world without loss, without regret, without sin. Can you tell me that orienting yourself towards the goal of their removal is evil?

Chapter 5: The Paradox and its Elimination

Those imagining falsehoods, a world where death (and taxes) do not exist, are suffering. Dissociated from our reality but associated with God's reality. If this is our new definition of suffering, then suffering is no evil. It is not negative. It is the path to truth and beauty. It's the acceptance of what is real and the evolution of the adult mind. To choose suffering is to want heaven where it is not, but to accept suffering will bring you into a divine state of being. This definition strips away the passive, victim connotation, and turns it into an active decision. It is at that moment you are more like God than any other. Where God watches his children in a place he would rather them not be, we watch our fellow men, children, and animals in a place they should not be. Maybe suffering is a transcendental, the one that belongs not to God, but to man? Where transcendentals separate God from man, suffering separates man from animal.

To live fully in the moment is to choose not to suffer, but this is not the same as choosing goodness. Suffering is not pain; pain is life. Suffering is the act of imagining yourself in a better state than the one you currently inhabit, of striving toward what ought to be. To reject this vision in favor of comfort is not evil, but it is neutral. It is the submission to reality as it is, not as it should be. Submission is not sin. It is peace, yes but not transcendence. This kind of peace does not make us more human; it makes us more like animals. Suffering is the fire in man that no beast can feel. It is what separates the human soul from the merely living. In this light, suffering is not to be avoided. It is to be understood, embraced, and honored, for it reveals that man was made for more than the world he inhabits.

Those who suffer rightly do so because they long for what ought to be. They are not rejecting reality, but affirming a deeper one. They are discontented, not with existence itself, but with its fracture. This is not the same as those who deny nature and reality altogether, those who claim men can bear children or that beauty is merely subjective. That is not suffering. That is evil. Evil is not the presence of longing, but the rejection of order. It denies Truth, calling falsehood wisdom. It denies Goodness, insisting that nature is tyranny. It denies Beauty, replacing harmony with chaos. Evil does not suffer because it does not strive but attempts to reshape the world in its own image and calls it peace. Suffering, by contrast, is the soul's resistance to disorder, a divine disquiet. It proves that man was made for more. It is not a flaw to be fixed; it is a compass pointing home.

This modern confusion between suffering and evil is cowardice dressed in compassion. It is intellectual laziness shielded by emotionalism. It may have not been accomplished intentionally, but it was achieved through decades and centuries of self coddling lies, terrified that meaning might demand something of them. Meaning always demands. Suffering is the demand. Evil, on the other hand, asks only that you surrender your reason, deny your nature, and call it love.

Chapter 6

The Problem of Evil

"The ancient man approached God as the accused person approaches his judge. For the modern man, the roles are reversed: he is the judge, God is in the dock."

-C.S. Lewis

The conclusion of this book is decisive and harsh. No more meandering debates. No more childish demands for a universe in which suffering, or rather living, does not exist. The so-called "problem of evil" is not a genuine objection to the divine; it is a tantrum thrown by the modernist, petulantly stomping their feet at a reality it cannot control. It is not theology. It is not even philosophy. It is despair dressed in the language of reason. It fails against the traditional definition and is incoherent with my postulated definition. If one cannot stomach living, one does not seek truth but instead seeks a fairy tale.

The problem of Evil: If God is good, why does he allow suffering and evil?

The implicit assumption here is that suffering is a negative. As we have demonstrated, suffering is good. Suffering is a mindset that orients us to the greatest good. It doesn't exist without cause because it only exists when a person chooses to enter it. It is not acted upon us, but is a thought we decide to have. There is no unnecessary suffering—a perception of a world that does not exist in this realm but does exist. It is the avenue through which the most Good can be accomplished. It is the struggle of a being that yearns for perfection yet remains bound by limitation. In this limitation, the greatest of good can be achieved. To argue that suffering disproves God is to argue that hunger disproves food, or that thirst disproves water. The very fact that we feel suffering affirms that there is something beyond our reach, something greater. That is not an argument against God. It is an argument for Him.

This question is malformed. It affirms the assumptions about what suffering is, about what evil is, and about what the nature of God must be. It presumes that pain and injustice disprove the divine. It assumes that the presence of discomfort cancels the presence of God. This is not logic, but entitlement.

The rejection of suffering is a rejection of responsibility. It is the demand of a spoiled child who wishes to be cradled rather than challenged. It is intellectual cowardice masquerading as sophistication. Those who espouse the problem of evil do not seek to understand God; rather, they seek to accuse Him, to place Him on trial before their own feeble understanding. How arrogant. How weak.

The true problem is not suffering. The true problem is that modern man has lost his ability to bear suffering with dignity. He has exchanged endurance for entitlement, fortitude for fragility. He does not seek wisdom but anesthesia. In this pursuit, he has made himself weak, lost, and unable to grasp the deeper reality of existence.

Suffering does not disprove God. It reveals Him. It strips away illusion, forces the soul to confront itself, and draws it toward the ultimate truth. Those who accept suffering do not fall into despair; they rise from the ashes. Those who reject suffering do not escape it; they merely diminish themselves in the process. They weakly blow away as the ash in the wind.

Theodicy does not need to explain away suffering; it needs to reclaim it as part of divine order.

Evil, well that is a construct of man, not God. It takes peculiar arrogance to demand a painless world, then call it evil when it doesn't obey. Evil simply doesn't exist in just the same manner dark, cold, and ignorance does not exist. Dark is a linguistically simple manner to explain the absence of light. One does not measure darkness; one measures the quantity of light and determines the lack thereof. Men cannot measure the cold; they measure the thermal energy and cold was added to our lexicon to distinguish when that thermal energy is below the point of human comfort. Ignorance, by its very definition, is the absence of knowledge. Do we take ignorance tests? It is just the same with evil, for we cannot measure an act's evilness. We can measure to what degree an act achieves the purpose that is in alignment with its nature. At the point to which an act goes against its very nature, then that act is simply without good, colloquially, evil.

A lion is not evil for killing the gazelle. The thermal vent is not evil for boiling a lobster. Man is not evil for being ignorant. Man is evil when he denies the fabric that makes up reality. When he denies Goodness, Truth, and Beauty. When he denies God. Without evil, the ability to choose good no longer exists. Without the presence of the possibility of evil, man has no contrast with the good. Art has no varying degrees of brightness, science is known and adventure lost, Goodness isn't a choice; it is a calculation. We are then not humans with free will choosing goodness, but animals simply existing. Lacking the image of God.

Let us recall the argument laid forth in this book: suffering is not evil. It is good. Suffering is not pain. Pain is the body reacting to external stimuli. Suffering is a chosen action of the mind. It is the act of imagining a world more rightly ordered than the one presently perceived. It is the mental, moral, and spiritual ache for what ought to be. It is the conscious movement toward Truth, Beauty, and Goodness, towards the transcendentals that exist eternally in God. Therefore, suffering is not a defect of creation; it is a signal that man was made for more. It is not a problem to be solved. It is a mystery to be embraced.

Thus, it is only the human that can be evil. It is only the human that can choose to turn its back on the transcendentals. If it is only the human that can be evil, to remove evil would be to remove the human. God, in His infinite mercy, has chosen instead to redeem us. The problem of evil, therefore, is not a problem. It is the greatest evidence we have that we are meant for more. That this world is not our home. That we were made in the image of the Divine, and that in our very longing we prove the reality of what we long for. To suffer is to strive. To strive is to rise. And to rise is to return to the One from whom all Goodness, all Truth, and all Beauty flows. Thus, we return to the question of this chapter: If God is good, why does He allow evil?

For he:

> allows man.
> allows freedom.
> allows greatness.
> allows love.

The Arguments

Disclaimer: The Problem of Evil is not an argument against the existence of God. It is not the foundational obstacle in the question of divinity; it is not a first-step objection. Rather, it is an objection to the existence of a loving, good, and interactive God. A God who is not only present, but also personally involved in human affairs.

Before one can meaningfully wrestle with the Problem of Evil, one must already accept or at least seriously entertain the existence of some form of God. This would typically be established through classical philosophical arguments such as:

- The Ontological Argument (Anselm, Descartes)
- The Cosmological Argument (Aquinas, Leibniz)
- The Teleological Argument (design, order, fine-tuning)
- Experiential and existential reasoning

The Problem of Evil does not challenge whether something divine exists; rather, it questions what kind of God exists. Specifically, it aims at the Christian conception of a God who is omnipotent, omniscient, and omnibenevolent.

This clarification is critical. You cannot reject divinity or deities on the basis of the Problem of Evil. In fact, there are many proposed deities that are quite evil. In that light, the Problem of Evil is not an atheistic argument in its essence, but a theological critique of the Judeo-Christian God.

The following is not a defense of God's existence in general, but a dismantling of the idea that suffering is incompatible with the God who is not only real, but Good, True, and Beautiful. It assumes the convincing debate on a supernatural creator has already been accomplished.

The Logical Problem of Evil

The assertion: If God is all-good and all-powerful, evil should not exist.

Historical Argument: This assumes we are more knowledgeable than God. That we know better than God. It assumes that, as a matter of fact, life would be better if the option for Evil didn't exist. It assumes that we know the totality of existence and all possible scenarios.

New Argument: A new argument isn't needed. The total lack of humility, the utter arrogance in this assertion is practically self-refuting.

The Evidential Problem of Evil

The assertion: There is too much suffering to justify belief in a good God.

Historical Argument: The historical argument falls much in line with the first one. It is extremely arrogant for us to believe that we know the proper amount of suffering. This argument weighs suffering as if it were measurable in units with equally measurable outcomes. This is simply false and hubristic.

New Argument: This presupposes that suffering is an evil. But if suffering is good, an orientation toward what is higher, then the very premise collapses. To remove suffering from the world would be to remove man's capacity to strive, to dream, to love. It would be to rip out the engine of the soul. A painless world is not a paradise; it is a prison. A world where no one suffers is a world where no one desires. If God is Good, then suffering must exist. It is not the contradiction of His nature, but the confirmation.

Suffering is the very mechanism by which man is drawn to the transcendent, thus the volume of suffering only reflects the depth of his hunger for the divine. To say there is "too much" suffering is to say there are too many people longing for what is better and beyond. The evidential problem does not indict God. It indicts our unwillingness to acknowledge that pain might serve a higher end. It reveals more about the cynicism and entitlements of man than it does the nature of God.

The Problem of Animal Suffering

The assertion: Animals suffer without moral or spiritual growth; therefore, suffering is gratuitous.

Historical Argument: This was probably one of the stronger arguments the Anti-Christian had, for the counterargument wasn't all that strong. It leaned somewhat on the argument that it was necessary, for without it there would be less overall Good. It also broke off into some heavily debated topics amongst Christians: Do animals have an afterlife? Do they have souls? Is there some afterlife benefit for them?

New Argument: Animals do not suffer. It is incoherent to say they do. They feel pain, but they do not suffer. Pain is physical. Suffering is metaphysical. A dog does not mourn its mortality. A deer does not despair over its fate. A lobster boiled alive may writhe in agony, but it does not dream of freedom or grieve its passing. Suffering requires imagination. It requires the concept of a better world, of a greater purpose. Animals cannot suffer because they cannot envision a reality other than the one they inhabit. This is the dividing line between man and beast. To suffer is to be human. If we are shown that an animal does have such ability or evolves to such a state, then we must simply believe that God will do for them what he has done for us.

It is similar to the argument for Aliens. It is not in our knowledge God's plan for them, but we can safely assume that he has some manner of justification and salvation. It is likely that the Story of Eden referenced in some degree the bestowment of the ability for introspection and therefore imagination. The ability for Adam to realize he was naked makes this evident.

The Problem of Natural Evil

The Assertion: Natural disasters and disease cause suffering indiscriminately.

Historical Argument: This argument refers back to other arguments in that we cannot know the totality of the effects of these storms and thus God found that the world could create more good with them than without them. For instance, much like video game developers inject troublesome events to give the characters a challenge and make the game worth playing, God allowed for such events to build character, resourcefulness, charity, etc.

New Argument: Nature cannot sin. It cannot rebel. It cannot turn away from Truth, Goodness, or

Beauty. It has no will. No capacity for moral failure. It simply is. To assign evil to nature is to misuse the term entirely. A hurricane is not evil. A virus is not a sinner. They operate according to the laws of a fallen world, but they do not defy God for they have no choice. Evil requires volition. It requires the ability to reject the Good. That is something only rational beings can do. Nature may break us, but it cannot betray us.

In fact, one may look at these events as good, for they are fulfilling their purpose in the most efficient manner possible, and it is in fact us that are evil for ignoring the Truth, Goodness, and Beauty in these events. We build by rivers, knowing they will flood to clean themselves out. We build in forests, knowing they must burn to revitalize themselves. We build on the sides of mountains, knowing gravity wants us to cascade down. We build on pristine beaches knowing that hurricanes will bring replenishing waters.

The Suffering of the Innocent

The Assertion: Children suffer without cause or consequence.

Historical Argument: This is the hardest argument to defeat. It is the most emotionally impactful. It is the one that every parent dreads, including myself. The thought of having to endure such trials quite literally takes your breath away. To attempt to even contemplate it raises your heart rate.

The traditional argument is that the most good comes from this suffering. It is the premise of the Book of Job, and through this act we are redeemed by Jesus. The motivations that arise from watching children die has led to many of the greatest human 'evolutions'. Dynamic shifts that have altered entire nations. The end of what many would refer to as the Industrial Revolution was enacted by many events including the sight and ending of child labor. The simple act of washing your hands became a scientific breakthrough because one scientist watched the death of mothers and their children.

New Argument: The historical argument still stands strong, but I'd offer a level of nuance. Even children possess the embryonic capacity for hope. They cry not merely from pain but from the awareness that things should be better. This awareness is the first

Chapter 6: The Problem of Evil

stirring of the transcendent within them. To weep is to know, even if dimly, that there is a Good worth longing for. That children can suffer is not a scandal. It is a sign that the *imago Dei* is already present in them.

Yet, it is often not the child who suffers the most. In fact, children tend to approach death with a poise far greater than the elderly. Their tiny hearts and minds are full of trust and acceptance. The transcendentals have not escaped them; they have not been corrupted. It is us watching who suffer the most. The parents who want to see their child grow in the descended and corrupted place. It is us who, one might say selfishly, believe in heaven and yet would rather our children continue to exist on the fallen earth so that we can experience it with them. It is us who want to see our children overcome broken arms and broken hearts. It is us who want to see how our children will pave their way to success or failure in life. It is us who want to give them a chance to achieve goodness in a place we know is full of the potential for evil. Just as God wants to see with each and every one of us. It is our tiny, tiny slice where we get to imagine how

God feels watching us. A correlation with the divine, as if we are made in the image of God.

About the Author

Keithen Hamilton is a Catholic, a devoted husband since the age of fifteen, and the father of four boys. *The Suffering Paradox* was not something he set out to write—it emerged from a deep, inescapable inner compulsion. After much prayer and reflection, he came to believe he was called to write this book for those who carry the quiet, persistent weight of daily suffering.

While many books address catastrophic loss, few speak to the unseen struggles—those who must rally themselves just to face each day. Hamilton writes for the ones who minimize their pain with thoughts like, "My suffering is nothing compared to my ancestors," "Toughen up, this is what it means to be a man," or "It's not about you; it's about your family." He speaks to those who, day after day, pray for change or simply for an end.

Though born and raised Catholic, Hamilton spent more than a decade exploring atheism and agnosticism, wrestling deeply with the problem of suffering. What began as a search for religious truth became an extended study of suffering itself, including five months focused solely on understanding pain and its role in the human experience.

What he found was unexpected: suffering is not to be avoided but embraced as a uniquely human path to Truth, Beauty, and Goodness. This book shares that discovery, challenging the prevailing view of suffering and inviting readers to recognize the divine in what is so often dismissed or feared.

www.ingramcontent.com/pod-product-compliance
Lightning Source LLC
Chambersburg PA
CBHW070853050426
42453CB00012B/2177